# MATT RE[DMAN]

MW00592628

## YOUR GRACE FINDS ME

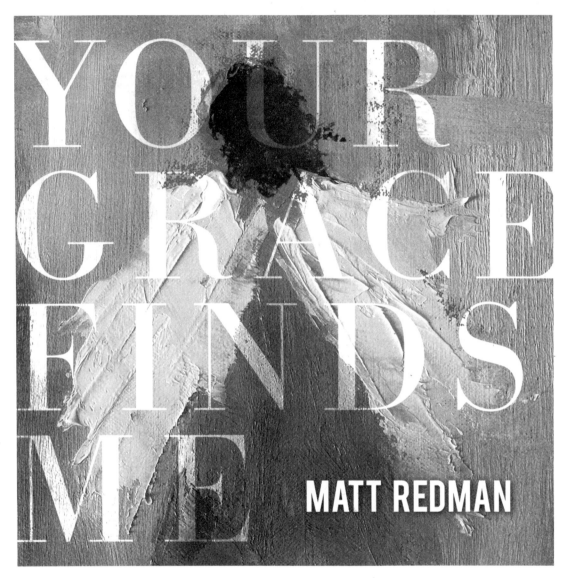

YOUR GRACE FINDS ME

**MATT REDMAN**

**AVAILABLE PRODUCTS:**

| | |
|---|---|
| Choral Book | 45757-2420-7 |
| CD Preview Pak | 45757-2420-1 |
| Listening CD | 45757-2420-2 |
| Split-Track Accompaniment CD | 45757-2420-3 |
| Audio .Wav Files DVD-ROM | 45757-2420-4 |
| (Praise Band/Strings) | |
| Orchestration/Conductor's Score CD-ROM | 45757-2420-8 |
| Rhythm/Chord Charts | 45757-2420-9 |
| (Rhythm, Chord Charts, Drum Set and String Reduction) | |
| Soprano Rehearsal Track CD | 45757-2421-0 |
| Alto Rehearsal Track CD | 45757-2421-5 |
| Tenor Rehearsal Track CD | 45757-2421-6 |
| Bass Rehearsal Track CD | 45757-2421-7 |
| Drum Rehearsal Track CD | 45757-2421-1 |
| Bass Guitar Rehearsal Track CD | 45757-2421-2 |
| Guitar Rehearsal Track CD | 45757-2421-3 |
| Piano/Keyboard Rehearsal Track CD | 45757-2421-4 |

**INSTRUMENTATION:**

| | |
|---|---|
| Flute 1, 2 | Violin 1, 2 |
| Oboe | Viola |
| Clarinet 1, 2 | Cello |
| F Horn 1, 2 (Alto Sax) | Bass |
| Trumpet 1, 2 | Synth String Reduction |
| Trumpet 3 | Rhythm |
| Trombone 1, 2 (Tenor Sax/Baritone T.C.) | Drum Set |
| Trombone 3, 4 | Chord Charts |
| Percussion | |

## WWW.BRENTWOODBENSON.COM

BENSON MUSIC PUBLICATIONS  a division of  BRENTWOOD-BENSON music publications

# CONTENTS

# Sing and Shout

Words and Music by
MATT REDMAN, JORGE MHONDERA
and WILLIE WEEKS
*Arranged by Cliff Duren*

3

© Copyright 2013 Thankyou Music (PRS) (Administered worldwide at CapitolCMGPublishing.com excluding Europe which is administered at wearworship.com) / worshiptogether.com Songs / Sixsteps Music / Said and Done Music (ASCAP) (Administered at CapitolCMGPublishing.com) / David Platz Music Inc. (BMI) (Administered by The Royalty Network, Inc.). All rights reserved. Used by permission.
**PLEASE NOTE: Copying of this music is NOT covered by the CCLI license. For CCLI information call 1-800-234-2446.**

prais - es out.__ We will__ sing and shout, yeah,

sing and shout! O - pen up our hearts and pour Your

prais - es out! Oh!__ Oh!__

11

**12**

**20**

that leads us home and makes a way? What could be bet-ter than Your great love?

# Your Grace Finds Me

Words and Music by
MATT REDMAN and JONAS MYRIN
*Arranged by Cliff Duren*

grace! Your great grace, oh, such grace!

The same for the rich and＿ poor,＿

the same for the saint and for the sin-ner,

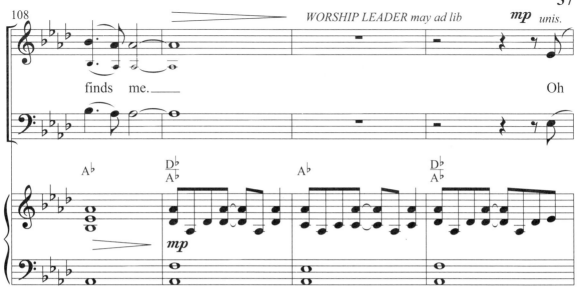

finds me. Oh

Your grace finds me.

Oh

# Mercy
## *with* Jesus Paid It All

Words and Music by
MATT REDMAN and JONAS MYRIN
*Arranged by Cliff Duren*

**40**

42

44

48

*(Optional Scripture Reading)*

Praise be to the God and Father of our Lord Jesus Christ! In his great mercy he has given us new birth into a living hope through the resurrection of Jesus Christ from the dead, and into an inheritance that can never perish, spoil or fade —

*(1 Pet 1:3-4a NIV)*

50

# I Need You Now

Words and Music by
MATT REDMAN, JONAS MYRIN
and SCOTT LIGERTWOOD
*Arranged by Cliff Duren*

52

54

# This Beating Heart

Words and Music by
MATT REDMAN and JONAS MYRIN
*Arranged by Cliff Duren*

**66** *CHOIR*

68

96

my soul sings for You!_____ This

99

beat-ing heart; I was made, I was made for You! My God, ev-er-

102

more, ev-er-more my soul,_____ my soul

44 **Optional Tag**
*W.L. ad lib*

**Optional Tag**

My soul,_____ my soul

sings for You!_____

# One Name Alone

Words and Music by
MATT REDMAN, JONAS MYRIN
and JASON INGRAM
*Arranged by Cliff Duren*

Ev-'ry-bod-y prais-es the thing they love.

**86**

**88**

**90**

Je-sus, be my ev-'ry-thing! Je-sus, be my ev-'ry-

thing! Je-sus, be my ev-'ry-thing!

# Jesus, Only Jesus

Words and Music by
CHRIS TOMLIN, MATT REDMAN,
CHRISTY NOCKELS, KRISTIAN STANFILL,
NATHAN NOCKELS and TONY WOOD
*Arranged by Cliff Duren*

You will com-mand the high-est praise! Yours is the Name
a - bove all names! You stand a - lone! I stand a - mazed!
Je - sus, on - ly Je - sus.

# Wide as the Sky

Words and Music by
MATT REDMAN, KRISTIAN STANFILL
and JONAS MYRIN
*Arranged by Cliff Duren*

WORSHIP LEADER

Hands up, hearts o-pen wide as the sky.___ We lift You high!

We lift You high! Hands up, hearts o-pen wide as the sky.

**112**

*lift Your name high!___ Our God,___ we lift You high!*

*We lift You high! Hands up, God, we*

*lift Your name high!___ Let all the oth-er names fade a-*

Lyrics:

84 — way. Let all the oth-er names fade a-way un-til there's on-ly

87 CHOIR — You. Let all the oth-er names fade a - way. Je - sus, take Your

89 — place. Je - sus, take Your place.

# Good Forever

Words and Music by
MATT REDMAN, REUBEN MORGAN
and JASON INGRAM
*Arranged by Cliff Duren*

From the be-gin-ning to ev-er-last-ing,

Your kind-ness knows no_____ end._____

And should the earth shake, should ev-'ry star fade,

**124**

126

**130**

# Let My People Go

Words and Music by
MATT REDMAN, GARY BAKER,
JONAS MYRIN and BETH REDMAN
*Arranged by Cliff Duren*

Light a fire in the dark,___ a fire in the dark!

Let my peo - ple go!_____

*CHOIR and WORSHIP LEADER*

Let my peo - ple go!_____

138

**142**

WORSHIP LEADER

An - oth - er sto - len life, an - oth - er hid - den cry.

These are Your sons___ and daugh - ters, God.

These are Your sons___ and daugh - ters, God.

**144**

Traf-ficked in the night, bro-ken by the fight.

We hear the cry:___ Let my peo - ple go!

Let my peo - ple go!

**148**

150

# Come and See

Words and Music by
MATT REDMAN, CHRIS TOMLIN,
JASON INGRAM and MATT MAHER
*Arranged by Cliff Duren*

155

**158**

hearts and lives wak-ing up to the Light of the world.

You're the Light of the world!____ God, it's Your

love here on dis - play. We stand in

159

awe! It takes our breath a-way!

Em7     D

Come and see.    Come and see what God has__ done.

A       E/G#

Come and see.    Come and see what love has__ won.

F#m7    D2

to the Light of the world.  You're the Light of the world!

You're the Light of the world!

164

# Benediction

Words and Music by
MATT REDMAN and JONAS MYRIN
*Arranged by Cliff Duren*

**170**

Fa - ther, the Spir-it and the Son. Oh

You will keep in perfect peace him whose mind is steadfast, because he trusts in you. *(Isaiah 26:3 NIV)*

LORD, you establish peace for us; all that we have accomplished you have done for us. *(Isaiah 26:12 NIV)*